Copyright © 2024 Wildmark Publishing

All rights reserved. This book or any portion thereof may not be reproduced or used in any manner whatsoever without the express written permission of the publisher, except in the case of brief quotations embodied in a review and certain other non commercial uses permitted by copyright law.

Paperback ISBN: 978-1-915834-39-3
Hardcover ISBN: 978-1-915834-40-9

Text by Becky Hemsley
Illustrations by Siski Kalla

Cover design and typesetting by Andy Harwood

First Edition, 2024

A Billion Dreams

BECKY HEMSLEY   SISKI KALLA

You know how the night sky holds billions of stars?
Burning and shining whenever it's dark?

Well, what if I told you, it's not as it seems?
That they're actually

billions

and

billows

of dreams

And each, every night when you climb into bed,

The dreams that you have all float out of your head.

Up past the trees and then up through the clouds,
Up to the night without making a sound

They meet with the moon and get ready to shine
Finding their place in the indigo sky

And that's where they watch, that's where they wait
Until it's their moment, their time and their place

Some stars are tiny and some stars are huge
See, if the star's big then the dream must be too

The wonderful thing is that when we are small
Our dreams are the greatest and wildest of all

The sky holds no limit to how far we'll soar
We'll dream to the stars then a little bit more

But sometimes your mind might be noisy and bright
And you might be finding it hard to sleep tight

And if that does happen, just look to the sky
Look at those stars that are all standing by

And search for the dreams all belonging to you
Just biding their time until they can come true

Then close your eyes tightly and promise me this
Never stop dreaming, and always dream...

My Big Dreams

Some people dream of becoming really good at something, a great writer or chef, a scientist or footballer! Others might dream of exploring the world or even outer space, while others might dream of cozy rainy days reading books, or snuggling with a pet, or perhaps sharing a laugh with someone special. Some might dream of helping animals or others in need. You might dream of living by the sea, in a cabin in the woods or perhaps with a friend in a city skyscraper! What are YOUR dreams? Draw or write your dreams on these clouds. Make a note of the date, so you can read them again when you're older and compare your new dreams with these!

www.ingramcontent.com/pod-product-compliance
Lightning Source LLC
LaVergne TN
LVHW071652060526
838200LV00029B/440